Warrior Of Wisdom

GOLDEN RAY OF LIGHT

Cleanse, Protect & Shine Your Light

Helen Lauritzen

Cover, Illustrations and Interior Design by Helen Lauritzen.

The author of this book does not dispense medical advice or prescribe the use of any technique as a form of treatment for physical, emotional, or medical problems without the advice of a physician, either directly or indirectly. The intent of the author is only to offer information of a general nature to help you in your quest for emotional, physical, and spiritual wellbeing. In the event you use any of the information in this book for yourself, the author and the publisher assume no responsibility for your actions.

DEDICATION

To my parents who have enriched my life with lessons,
Wisdom and golden memories.

Thank you for your endless love and support,
always encouraging me to shine my Light. ❤

CONTENTS

INITIAL REMARKS

We are an astonishing race of exceptional talents and imagination. No other species on this planet is able to create such mind-blowing constructions, technical contraptions and social intelligence (evolved social beliefs and attitudes), that has spanned over many generations.

Yet we are also the most destructive of all species to our environment and other species, whether they are animals or plants on land or in the depths of our oceans. Most disappointingly we are destructive to our own kind. This is our biggest downfall and there are those among us that are willing to 'serve' and clean up the mess, that so many before us and those here today continue to create, in order for our Earth to return to the Garden of Eden that it once was.

We, as a species, can do so much more for our kind, and all those that live and breathe in this magnificent world that we live in. We are uniting as Warriors of Wisdom, standing tall and embracing our gifts and talents that can only make positive changes if we just continue to keep all our Wisdom secure and strong, nurturing our Pearls of Wisdom to raise our self-belief, resilience, and courage to their highest levels, vibrating a positive energy full of love, compassion, and acceptance of Self and others.

With a strong mindset, sifting through the 'white noise' and only accepting that which is true to our Core and that which supports our Dreams and Soul Purpose, we are able to move forward. Thus we have a duty of care to ourselves to ensure that our Spirit continues to rise and soar so that we are the best version of ourselves that we can be by serving Mother Earth and all her species, her children, so that we can live in harmony once again.

We have come to realize that it is extremely important to be strong in our ability to keep a positive mindset because we are unable to attract positive situations and people if our mind, body, and spirit are not positively charged. We need constant 'training' to keep our mind, our troublesome and doubting Ego, in cooperation with our heart and Soul, forever reminding ourselves to see the lesson within the negative, to nurture it and create the Pearl that is then added to our Wisdom. It is this Wisdom that guides us to make decisions, constantly sifting through all information, situations, and people as to what stays in our Story and what is discarded.

We need to focus on keeping our mind, body, and spirit in optimum functioning condition so that we can continue to move forward on our path. This means we need to cleanse our internal energy as well as protect it from the negative energies that continue to swirl around us.

We also need to stay focused on all that brings us joy and gratitude, what lights us up, to continue keeping our mind in a happy place so that it cooperates with all parts, especially our internal barometer - our gut instinct. This is quite crucial for us to succeed in all that we dream to be.

There is so much we can do to make a difference, combining as *Warriors of Wisdom* bathing in the *Golden Ray of Light* that fills our Core, our Spirit, and our Inner Warrior. We just need to practice but a few different techniques that will clear the negativity in ourselves and our environment (home, school, or work) as well as continue to learn to strengthen our mindset, intuition and immune system to combat disease (dis-ease).

There is no right or wrong to the methods you choose to practice, only to make a promise of good faith to use them wisely and honestly for the good of all concerned, making peace and harmony our *intentions* at all times.

Remember, you deserve to feel

safe and free

loved and honored

strong and courageous

creative and intuitive

at all times.

Take these methods and join them with your

gifts and talents

strengths and weaknesses

mind and soul

always believing that you are worthy and you are enough. You are so giving and talented in so many ways.

Let your Light shine far and wide, let your Voice be heard loud and clear, let your love be felt with warmth and compassion, and may you always stand tall and proud in the Golden Ray of Light.

1 KEEPING OUR MINDSET POSITIVE

N ow that you have read book one in the Warrior of Wisdom series, 'No Grit, No Pearl', you have come to understand just how important it is to keep your mind and Soul positive by listening to our inner Voice that carries so much Wisdom from our Ancient One, always guiding us and keeping us on our Soul Path.

We have come to learn the importance of the words we choose, especially those that start with 'I am'.

We have come to understand just how important it is to incorporate the 4 principles (Survival, Compassion, Forgiveness, and Acceptance) into our life to create a ripple effect of kindness and self-confidence back into our world.

We can give so much to ourselves in the way of self-belief and self-nurturing by accumulating our Pearls of Wisdom.

We must continue to strengthen our Inner Warrior and feed them with Wisdom to be the best version of ourselves.

This is the first stage of becoming our ultimate being, here to serve a purpose for the good of all mankind. We just have to keep these tools of Wisdom in practice so we can continue to access and encourage our gifts and talents, moving towards our Soul Purpose. We can only succeed if we keep our mindset full of strength, courage, resilience, and unlimited creativity with endless possibilities. This is what we are all striving to fulfill in this lifetime and many to come, depending on what you believe.

The second stage is to heal ourselves from the inside. Clearing all that is negative and toxic to our selves, to our Soul and to our Inner Child who is so loving and curious to explore life. It is this stage that we need to start to understand better so we can keep ourselves healthy in mind, body, and spirit. We are always subjected to so much negativity in various environments that we need to know what methods we can use to protect our energy from the unhealthy energy of others as well as fuel our vessel, our only body to our existence on this Earth during this lifetime, and keep it well-nourished so it can perform at an optimum level. This is so crucial to us being able to fulfill our Purpose as it is vital to remove all blocks from our natural flow of Source or Spirit, the energy from the Universe.

You are an amazing being with so much potential to move mountains in so many ways.

You are an instrument of profound change and inspiration.

You are a magnificent work of art in the making.

But we cannot be all of this if we do not take care of our body, our vessel, our ship that is transporting us along the flow of our path. We cannot thrive if what we consume or subject ourselves to what is not conducive to our optimum level of health. We cannot function at all if the nuts and bolts to our ship have deteriorated, leaving holes and not allowing our parts to integrate and flow in unison. Just like a well-maintained ship carrying precious cargo, we have a duty to care for all parts of our ship, making sure it is sea-worthy or should we say worthy of our Soul, our inner Child, and the Warrior within. We have a duty of care to make sure that we keep our ship *clean and fuelled* well so we are prepared and able to endure whatever may facilitate or obstruct our path along our amazing journey.

To keep our vessel clean and to keep it fuelled is also the essence of Principle 1 – Survival. We cannot be the ultimate Warrior of Wisdom if we do not care for ourselves. We must place our health and wellbeing at the top of our list of priorities, for we are only able to assist others if we are nourished and stable. If our vessel is full to nurture ourselves first, we are then able to give to others. We cannot give if we are empty and with nothing to give. It just cannot be.

So it is time to learn how we can keep our vessel in ultimate condition and embrace the Golden Ray of Light throughout our daily practices.

2 GOLDEN RAY OF LIGHT

So what is the Golden Ray of Light? You are in the healing and divine presence or Source, God, Spirit, or the Universe (whatever your belief) when you step into the Golden Ray of Light. When you step into this golden beam it can either protect you or it can cleanse and heal you. No matter what your preference, it is easy to access simply through your ability to *visualize* and your capacity to set your *intention* from a place of Love.

This Golden Ray of Light is so warm, like the rays of our sun, feeding our Soul with nutrients on a physical and spiritual level. It is able to penetrate our body to the Core of our being and can fill every cell in our body to help us release all toxins, negativity, and distress that we have accumulated from our day to day activities. We have the ability to dissipate all that is not required, all the unhealthy energies that we have absorbed, by accessing the Golden Ray of Light. It is a pure and loving energy from God, our Creator, the Universe that can give us so much in the way of healing and protection . . . and more.

When we look at the properties of the gold metal found on our planet, it is scientifically classified as a "noble metal", which means it is a pure and non-reactive metal that does not tarnish or corrode. It is also the only metal of this color which is why the Ancient People of long ago and those of today value it.

Gold has also been used in medicine to treat diseases throughout the history of ancient and modern civilization dating back to the Chinese in 2500BC and to the Ancient Egyptians who also believed it attracted positive energy and is a great healing mineral. In recent times, we have used it to effectively treat various forms of arthritis and in dental care, and it is now being tested to treat cancer patients.

In metaphysics, it is no wonder that gold has been known as "the master healer". It has been reported to have a warm, calming, and balancing vibration that is known to increase circulation and relaxation. This aids the body's natural balancing process to stabilize the emotional, digestive, hormone, and blood systems, which isn't surprising considering that our bodies contain approximately 0.2 milligrams of gold and most of it in our blood. This, in turn, adds to the notion that it provides composure, alleviates tension and stress, and amplifies positive feelings.

The Golden Ray of Light is also pure, just like the gold found within the depths of this Earth. It can dissolve all that is toxic inside us and around us, therefore it has the capacity to heal and protect at all times, balancing our energy fields especially the energy within our heart. It is a matter of allowing it into your heart and your Soul, and making an allowance in our minds for the possibility that it can.

You are the master of your cells, your body, your ship. This source of healing and protection is so beneficial to keeping your vessel, your body clean, and fuelling it well so that you stay on your path. It is a source of good and loving energy that can only guide you to safer waters. It has the capacity to keep you calm, in balance, and in such a peaceful state of mind. You just have to have an *open* mind and be *willing* to use it.

As Albert Einstein said, *"Everything is energy"* including our *thoughts*. Everything we do is fuelled by our *intention*, good or bad. We have the potential to live in peace and harmony, surrounded by good people and situations if we truly believe that this is what we want and is best for our wellbeing. And we know that this could only be what our inner Child would want, always wanting what is best for us.

So as we continue to set our intentions from a place of love and compassion (Principal 2) we continue to increase the effectiveness of our Golden Ray of Light, so beautiful and warm, full of love and peace, complete in its ability to heal and protect.

This Golden Ray of Light is the key to our ability to function in a world that is so consumed by Ego, negative energy, and foods that are so riddled with chemicals and genetically modified.

This Golden Ray of Light is the Source that will help your inner Warrior to survive.

3 OUR ENERGY, OUR FORCE

Everything is energy. Everything has its own vibration, whether it is animal, vegetable, or mineral. We all emit our own unique vibration and many of us have experienced this at one time or another. We have sensed when there is tension between two people who have been arguing, even by simply walking into a room they are in, and when they suddenly become quiet. We have sensed someone's sadness even though they may not show signs of crying. We have sensed someone's anger towards us even if they may not be yelling or have an angry face. All these feelings that we can sense from another is an indication of their internal energy that they are emitting.

Some people's energy can be good especially when they are feeling happy or excited, or even calm and at peace when sitting within the beauty of Nature. Others can be quite angry or aggressive. They can even be people that we go to school with, work with, or live with. Being exposed to negative energy in large doses will result in that energy resonating with our energy and therefore can be quite toxic.

To explain resonance, a classic example is breaking a glass with sound waves emitted from a tuning fork. If the tuning fork is struck at the right pitch and placed next to a wine glass, its resonating frequency or energy can fracture or even shatter the glass. This is because a wine glass has a natural resonance, that being a frequency, at which the glass will vibrate easily. Therefore the glass can be moved by the sound wave at that particular frequency. If the force from the sound wave making the glass vibrate is big enough, the size of the vibration will fracture the glass.

Toxic energy in large doses from negative people has the same affect on our energy. Our energy picks up the vibration of their energy and, though it won't shatter our body, our energy begins to emulate their vibration until we begin to internalize their negative energy or emotions as our own. This is why we can sometimes feel anxious, upset, or angry for no *apparent* reason. If this is a re-occurring pattern for you, then it is highly likely that you are extremely sensitive to other people's emotions, an empath, and are most definitely affected by their energy whether it is positive or negative.

For empaths, it is important to protect ourselves from negative energy. As we know, negative energy dissociates our amazing parts that make us whole. Nothing good comes from negative energy, only more negativity. It disrupts our flow and can lead us off the path and away from our Soul Purpose.

Our energy is such a strong force. It affects everyone and everything around us and, in turn, it can be so affected by others to our detriment. It is a force worth protecting so we can function at our optimum as well as attract amazing and good things into our life.

We project our energy in so many ways from the words we speak, the thoughts we think, and the feelings we emit. We are able to create ripple effects within the energy that surrounds us. This is why we must keep our energy positive so that we emit positive energy to create a chain reaction of positivity around us. This can only be of benefit to our overall wellbeing.

We have so much power over our energy and can expand this ability by connecting to our infinite Source from the Universe, the Golden Ray of Light. We can use this beautiful energy to make a world that allows us to thrive and is for the good of all. It is our connection to one another and a force that allows us to be the best versions of ourselves that we can be. This force is our way of recharging our self so we continue to co-create our Story, our world. We have the capacity to change the ripple we create in the energy that surrounds us. We have the intensity to create our Dreams simply by adjusting our own energy. We just need to nurture and protect it.

4 GOLDEN BUBBLE OF PROTECTION

We can be surrounded by so many different energies at the one time, some good and some harmful to our energy. That is why it is so important to protect our energy and our Core where all our Divine Wisdom is stored. We can never assume that our energy is not going to be affected. To be sure, we can place a 'protective armor' around our physical self to keep our energy safe.

As we get dressed in the morning, it is at this point that we can also complete our dressing routine with our ritual of protection. We just need to make sure that we are not interrupted, so make sure you are alone when carrying out this method. This ensures the intention of protection will be set.

Once dressed, stand in a comfortable position and close your eyes. Allow yourself to relax as you breathe slowly and deeply, in and out, allowing yourself to be calm and peaceful. When ready, begin to visualize yourself inside of a big, golden bubble that surrounds all of you from head to toe. Set the intention with your thoughts that this bubble is very strong and impervious to any

negative or harmful energy. It can only let in good and loving energy. As you continue to stand inside your bubble, visualize a beautiful beam of golden light shining down from the Universe onto the top of your bubble. As it is a good and loving energy, it starts to flow inside your bubble filling all of the space inside. As it starts to touch your skin, it feels warm and soothing. As it starts to penetrate your skin and enter into your body, you feel so calm and peaceful as it fills every cell in your body.

When you feel that your body has reached its capacity to receive this golden light, be sure to set your intention of gratitude by saying a small prayer of thank you to the Universe for your protection for the day like this one:

Thank you for my strong Golden Bubble of Protection to shield me from all negative energies so I may continue to flow with love and compassion for the good of all.

It is all about the *intention* you set along with your visualization. You can also say an affirmation like this:

I am peaceful, powerful, and protected at all times.

This golden beam of light, the Golden Ray of Light, is your light of protection and the golden bubble your armor, both protecting you from the negative or toxic energies that might confront you during your day. They are there to protect your energy daily so it is important to visualize your golden bubble of protection every morning. Most of all, your prayer, affirmation, and your intention is what *seals* your golden bubble, your suit of armor.

This ritual has a lot of positive repercussions where you may start to repel all negativity, including people who are a detriment to your energy. Negative situations may start to become less and less. And you may start to attract more of what is positive into your life.

5 <u>DEEP CLEANSE</u>

Sometimes we can feel a little offbeat even when we have put our golden bubble of protection around us. It doesn't mean we didn't visualize very well or our intention was not set properly. It just means that the energy that we have come in contact with may have been an energy that was extremely harsh or toxic. This could be a person, or could even be harsh-sounding or distasteful music, or sometimes a disturbing item broadcasted on the news that has altered our positive and peaceful state without us being aware.

There were times when the Ancient Warriors failed to defend themselves despite their shining armor and weapon. It wasn't because they were unprepared. It just meant they were caught by surprise. This can happen to us as well when negative energy, in whatever form, comes into our Sacred Space. The way we can tell that this has happened is by noticing our body's Signs of discomfort. Signs from our body are such that we can have a headache, or we can feel irritable, upset, or even angry. However, the key to remember is that these signals from our body seem to occur for *no apparent reason*. This usually means that we have absorbed the energy from someone else that was emitting these same emotions and have internalized them as our own. They have seeped into our Core and can lead us out of the flow of positive and balanced emotions if we leave them in there for too long. So it is important that we remove them from our system, our Sacred Space, so we can begin to flow and be in harmony with ourselves once again.

When we detect our body's Signs of discomfort, we can call upon the Golden Ray of Light to cleanse our inner Core and our energy. This is another method that we can also easily incorporate into our daily routine, such as when we are taking a shower to cleanse our body at the end of the day.

> *As you stand under the gentle stream of warm water, close your eyes and allow the crown of your head to remain under it, allowing you to breathe comfortably as it flows over your face. Then visualize a Golden Ray of Light shining through the flow of water. It is a breathtaking vision as the water begins to sparkle and shimmer, a small waterfall of gold. This water is now charged with Divine Light, the same that we used for our bubble of protection, but now we are using it for cleansing and healing.*

> *As the golden water washes over your body you can then start to feel and visualize the negative energy or emotion that is inside your Sacred Space, your heart, as a dark and murky ball of gunk. Allow it to move away from your heart, past your ribs, and out through your skin. Visualize this dark ball of gunk or negative energy being washed down the outside of your body and down the drain, feeling your heart becoming lighter and your body becoming more and more relaxed with the soothing flow of golden water.*

As you continue to visualize this negative energy going down the drain, be sure to set your intention of gratitude by saying a small prayer of thank you to the Universe for removing all toxic energy that does not serve you for your highest wellbeing like the one below and a couple of affirmations to complete the ritual:

Thank you for releasing and clearing all negatives energies, thoughts, emotions, and beliefs from my mind, body, and spirit that no longer serve my wellbeing and Soul Purpose. Thank you for transmuting these lower energies to Love and Light.

I am cleansed and clear.

I only allow that which is for my highest good to enter within my Sacred Space.

This is a beautiful and calming technique to ensure your energy fields stay clean and it allows your mind, body, and spirit to continue to thrive in an internal environment of positivity, love, and light.

To cleanse our body of negative energy is so vital to our mental, physical and spiritual wellbeing so we can continue to keep ourselves whole and all our systems functioning and flowing with positive energy, keeping our vibration high. This cleansing takes our vibration to much higher planes of reception and fulfillment. It opens our vessel to receive the Wisdom from the Ancient Ones, allowing us to download our information, our road maps, and all that we need to move forward day after day. It is our Source of renewal for sustaining our positive mindset to fulfill our Purpose in life so that can share our positivity with others and continue the ripple effect of positivity, love, and compassion for all including ourselves.

We have a duty of care to ourselves to keep our vessel clean and in good working order.

We have a duty of care to ourselves to fill our mind, body, and spirit with love and all things good.

We have a duty of care to remove all that is toxic and to shun all that does not serve us.

We have a duty of care to learn and implement all that we can to keep our mind, body, and spirit healthy so that we remain strong, courageous, and resilient to the negativity that keeps trying to enter our Sacred Space.

When it comes to removing negativity, we can also remove negative self-limiting beliefs, whether they are imposed by others or self-imposed. We can also use the visualization of the Golden Ray of Light shining onto our food to remove toxins and chemicals we may have consumed that may not be good for our health. We can also visualize this Golden Light shining on an environment that has conflict or disharmony to reduce negativity amongst people and to assist with finding a solution to problematic situations. There is no limit to the use of this wonderful force of golden energy that we can use to remove all blocks from our natural flow of Source. It is all to do with our intention of its use and this intention coming from a place of Love.

We just have to strengthen our mind, keeping it in a routine of self-protection and cleansing. By training our mind to visualize and utilize the Golden Ray of Light in our newly applied routines, we are able to strengthen our mindset, intuition, and immune system. Making these techniques an integral part of our daily rituals allows us to keep radiating and attracting all that is beautiful, wonderful, amazing and good . . . for that is what we are.

6 TEMPLE OF GOLD

So now we are able to protect and cleanse our body's energy. This is in preparation for building our mindset to one of strength, power, and determination. We have a beautiful and creative mind, full of endless possibilities, capable of composing and executing so many different ideas. It is a valuable tool and if used well and nurtured well, it can make our Dreams become reality.

Yet there are times when we become overwhelmed with doubt, not trusting our inner Wisdom, our Ancient One. We cannot seem to see beyond our fears and become immobile with panic. We cannot hear our inner Voice giving us our next step, our next move to go forward. And so we continue to spiral down into negativity and develop a total lack of confidence. We lose access to our self-belief system, not remembering nor honoring our talents and our gifts that have not been lost, just temporarily forgotten, temporarily hidden from our mind, lost in a fog of confusion and despair.

There is a method that we can use to calm the mind so that it does not get in the way of our strength and

determination to succeed. It relies on your intention to 'serve' and be honorable, to give and love from your heart, and not be persuaded by a dominating and inflated Ego. It is a method that calls upon finding your true essence and will only be of benefit if that essence is fuelled with the strongest source of all . . . Love. Love has no negativity, no boundaries, or limitations. It is pure and cannot be measured for it is neither solid, liquid, or gas. It is pure energy, not tainted or disguised. It comes from Source, above and within. It can only guide us and serve us if our intentions are also good and pure. It is our connecting life force to our self and all parts . . . and to others.

Before we begin, make sure you are seated comfortably and there are no distractions around you. As you close your eyes, feel your breath slowing down and becoming deeper as you breathe in and breathe out, feeling your body relax and letting go of all tension.

> *Visualize a very tall and beautiful building of grand architecture in front of you. It appears to be a sacred temple. Its energy is calm and inviting. Its walls are gold with a slight shimmer in the sunlight, large columns from the ground to a vaulted rooftop on either side of a large golden door, intricate in design and full of beauty. As you grab and pull the big, gold handle on the door that is ornate with beautiful crystals, it opens without a sound. Yet, as you step inside this building there is soft, tranquil music from a harp being played that fills the silence.*

> *As you cast your eyes around the large room you notice that the floor, the walls, and the ceiling are also shimmering in gold as the Golden Ray of Light filters through a big open window in front of you. In the middle of the room, there are two large treasure chests. The one on the left seems to be quite old and covered in dust, quite plain in appearance. As you open the lid, so heavy and awkward, you look inside and you can see there is more dust and many things that make you feel uncomfortable, upset, and perhaps angry. They are memories of the past, especially your childhood. They are negative emotions, thoughts, and limiting beliefs. Take a good moment to make*

sure all of these negative energies are all inside . . . every single one. As you take one last look at these negative energies, thank them for the lessons learned from each of them. Then say to yourself:

"Because of you, I am able to nurture my Pearls of Wisdom."

"Because of you, I have learned that I am all that I am."

"I am enough."

"I am worthy."

Then visualize the Golden Ray of Light coming through the big window and streaming into this chest. As it touches all that is inside, they begin to dissolve and as they dissolve you feel calmer, your heart feels lighter and a sense of peace fills you. Continue visualizing these negative energies dissolving until there is nothing left in the chest. Once empty, you will now shut this chest.

As you turn your gaze toward the other treasure chest on the right, you see that it is golden in color, so beautifully ornate and shiny. You open the lid to look inside and it is very light and easy to lift. As you begin to lift its lid, a shaft of golden light escapes and floods the room. When you look inside you see that this chest is filled with beautiful and happy memories from the past and further into your childhood. All the things that make your heart sing, all your favorite things that make you joyful and light you up, all the things that fill you with Love. They are full of positive emotions, thoughts, and empowering beliefs. Take a moment to look at each item, feel their beauty and meaning to you . . . every single one.

As you look at these positive energies, thank them for the lessons learned from each of them. Then say to yourself:

"Because of you, I have learned that I am incredible in every way."

"I am a Warrior with great inner Wisdom."

"I am on the path to achieving my Soul Purpose."

"I will achieve my Dreams."

It is this treasure chest that we keep open . . . always.

It is this treasure chest that we go back to when we are deep in our Sacred Space, overflowing with the protective and healing Golden Ray of Light.

It is this treasure chest, so full and inspiring that we feel deep gratitude for . . . and Love.

It is this treasure chest that we continue to fill with positive emotions, thoughts, empowering beliefs, and our Pearls of Wisdom each time we come back and visit the building with the golden walls, the Temple of Gold.

This is the place that you can visit when you are deep in your Sacred Space at any time, especially when you feel like you are not going the right way, when nothing seems to be working out. When we are grateful for all that we have, and even for all that we wish to achieve, we attract more of the same into our lives. We begin to get back on track and into the flow. We start to change our energy to one of positivity, Love, and golden light. We start to create again, from the foundation of who we are, those bits and pieces that light us up and make our Spirit soar. This is what makes up our essence and, in turn, is used to fulfill our Purpose.

7 SACRED SPACE OF SOLITUDE

Our Sacred Space is our place of quiet, our place to consult our Inner Child and our Ancient One, the ying and yang of our Soul. It is a place where we can go to find the answers within, our Wisdom. We have a place to go to when we are confused and unable to move forward with a decision that is imperative to our path and even our wellbeing. This we know.

Our Sacred Space is also a place of solitude so that we can just rest and be still in silence. We need to embrace solitude daily so that we can become better at accessing our Inner Voice. We have so much to sift through and digest when the day is over. We are not machines just moving through our daily routine, day in and day out. We are so much more than this. We are beings of Light and creativity, here to fulfill our Purpose.

Time in solitude is a prerequisite to a calm and stable mind, the mind of a Warrior.

Warriors of ancient times would sit in quiet contemplation to prepare themselves for the hunt or even for battle. It was a ritual well-practiced, helping them to focus and address their task at hand. It helped them to fuel their belief that they were able to accomplish their task and also help them to go further into their Core to extract their innate Wisdom to create a plan of attack. Just by sitting in quiet solitude, and going into our Core, we can also access our deep inner Wisdom that allows us to create and evolve through constant sifting, evaluation, acceptance of what belongs to our Truth, and what will be the next step in our plan of attack, or chapter in our Story.

We are Warriors in our own right, trying to survive at all times, dealing with various situations, going into battle sometimes for ourselves, and sometimes for what we believe in. We are instinctively striving for what will benefit us and what will help us to succeed. We can only do this through consulting our internal barometer and our inner Wisdom within our place of solitude.

We have so much to gain in this place, our Sacred Space. We can send our intention to the Universe, to manifest our desires and Dreams with the vision of them appearing in our lives, and the gratitude that they will appear soon, at some point, in the not so distant future. We have the ability to create so much just through visualizing our Dreams and our plan of attack. We can imagine so many scenarios and possibilities that can manifest into opportunities to create our actual reality from what was once a Dream. In our place of solitude, we can feel, hear, see, taste, and smell our Dreams with uninterrupted vision. We can feel it all with our senses as if it were happening Now. It is when we can visualize our Dream and *feel* it, as if it were so very real, that it begins to manifest into reality. We can set the wheels in motion if we make sure that what we want to appear and happen in our lives is from a place of Love and a place of pure gratitude.

All we need to do from that point is to 'Let go and let God'. Let the energy flow out to the Universe and wait for it to come back. Our positive vibration of gratitude and Love continues to act as a magnet to those Dreams we feel in our Core, in our heart, and in our Soul. And when they do appear we must be even more grateful. This is part of the Universal Law of Manifesting for the good of all mankind. And like continues to attract like.

Our Sacred Place of Solitude is our hearth to forge our Dreams.

It is here that we sharpen and refine our tools, our gifts and our talents. It is here where we continue to strengthen our ability to listen to our Voice so that we can become the master of our thoughts . . . the Master of our Dreams.

8 GOLDEN PATH OF SYNCHRONICITY

There are many intriguing stepping stones that we must cross over as we travel our path, which vary with the experiences they hold. These stones start to merge into a beautiful picture of interconnected patterns that allow us to understand our Story full of lessons and synchronicity.

We can choose to stand on just one stone all our life, only to encounter very limited sights, sounds, and physical sensations so as not to get hurt in any way. This is the *safest* choice, but it is also quite a mind-numbing choice. If we choose to step on another stone, we can experience so much more and we ultimately increase our self-confidence by moving out of our comfort zone, ensuring our Ego that we have successfully moved to a different 'place' and we are still okay. No bumps, no bruises, no scrapes, no breaks. We are enjoying yet another moment of conquering our fears and claiming success.

Every step we take leads us closer to achieving our goals, our Dreams, and our Soul Purpose.

Every step we take becomes a lesson, a Pearl of Wisdom.

Every step we take allows us to strengthen our resilience, our confidence, and our Warrior within.

Every time we step out of our comfort zone we see another piece of the puzzle fit into place and our path starts to become clearer and more authentic. It opens up and does not seem so treacherous nor as unfamiliar as it did when we first started. Our inner Voice becomes louder, and the Signs become more frequent and recognizable, as though we are getting closer and closer to 'home'.

Our steps are governed by the decisions we make. Our decisions are governed by how we choose to 'see' the stepping stones that lay before us. We could choose to see them as treacherous and dangerous. We could allow our Ego to convince us that there is only doom and gloom if we continue to the next step, for sometimes we do have to pass through the storm, go through a maze or crawl through the mud to get to the next one. However, if we choose to rise to the challenge and we come out successful on the other side, this is what makes life so exciting, so interesting and *so satisfying*. And if we continue to find different solutions, we continue to train the Warrior within for whatever challenges life may give to us, for they are a gift, no matter how daunting, overwhelming or fearsome they *appear* to be. It is the Universe's way of saying:

"You are ready to tackle this one."

"You have all that you need to get through this and learn the lesson inside."

"You can be proud of all that you have achieved and move to the next step."

"You can add your Pearl to your golden treasure chest and be proud of who you are."

There will always be stepping stones, connected to one another with the experiences and lessons we are meant to endure or enjoy. And as we look at our path of stepping stones through the eyes of our inner Child, with excitement, wonder and a sense of adventure, we begin to see that we are following our inner Wisdom that has been lighting our way all along, shining ever so brightly, leading us along our Golden Path of Synchronicity, all people and all experiences coming together to further complete the puzzle. All we need to do is to step up and out of our emotions to see the bigger picture so we understand the road we have traveled, see where we are standing in the Now, and to continue to have the courage to take the next step that leads us closer to becoming who we are meant to be, to enjoy the moment, be happy and to shine as bright as we can along the way.

9 STANDING TALL, SHINING BRIGHT

It is in our nature to 'shine' and bring forward all our gifts and talents. It is neither natural nor beneficial to hide what we are *meant* to be.

All wild animals, and even the plants around us, shine in all that they are, never hiding, never doubting for they have not been *conditioned* to be anything else other then what they were put on this Earth to do. Yes, animals that have been domesticated have also been conditioned in varying degrees to behave and conform to how people train them to be. People are no different for they have been 'trained' to believe and behave how society wants them to be; whether it be cultural expectations or imposed rules appointed by various governing bodies, religious or social groups.

This is a pattern that we all need to break so we can become free in our way of thinking and feeling, free to be ourselves, more like the children of Mother Nature . . . untamed and limitless. It is up to us to think about all *learned* rules and expectations, as well as those to come, and dissect it all so that we sort *beneficial* from *restricting or harmful*, or that which is simply not needed.

We do not need to be in constant restraint with what others think we should or shouldn't do. We do not need to constantly conform, especially if we do not feel comfortable with the expectations others have for us. All we need to do is follow our heart, be kind to others as we travel on our journey and to allow what 'lights us up' to lead us, for what lights us up is where our talents and our inner gifts lie. It is here where we find out who we truly are. It is here where we begin to experiment with our talents, finding out the nuts and bolts of our ship and all it is capable of, finding the limitations and pushing them further.

There is no need to hide what makes us who we are for these are the parts that make us shine our most beautiful and amazing Light that leads us on our path, even when it appears to be dark sometimes.

We follow our path best when we embrace all our parts, all our strengths, weaknesses (if any), our gifts and our talents, all developing and evolving as we continue with courage and listen to our inner Voice, our Ancient One, and especially our inner Child with so much knowledge about who we really are.

Keep listening to your inner Child of wonder and amazement, for the courage to experiment, experience new things, and enlightenment will come from them. This is where our gifts and talents lie. This is where true happiness, enjoyment, and simply 'being' exist. This is how we discover what we like and what we don't like. This is how we 'see' ourselves and all that is happening around us with untainted pureness, innocence, and Love.

Our inner Child is not afraid to try, fail, and try again. Our inner Child does not overthink the process of experiencing something new. This part of us is extremely brave, dabbling in the new with all our senses. It is the driving force of what makes us step out of our comfort zone, mesmerized by what is possible if we simply just *try*. And when we do take that step and try, we discover so many things that we are capable of doing that we never knew we could do before. We start to build our repertoire of accomplishments, skills, and talents, having a greater understanding of our gifts and who we are.

We are all things that raise our vibration.

We are all things that inspire us to get up in the morning, to be all that we are and all that we can be.

We are that beautiful Source, that Golden Ray of Light that exists all around us.

We are all part of the Universe, Source, God, beaming so radiantly in every direction, which ultimately means we are creating so much love and compassion for ourselves and others. We have the power to allow our distinctive Light to shine. It is time we stand tall, time we shine and shine bright.

10 WHAT LIGHTS US UP

There has always been something, and sometimes quite a few things, that will light up the essence of our being right through to our Core. These are the things that tend to make our heart fill up with so much joy and even excitement, causing us to be on such a 'high' in emotions that are pure happiness and love for all the ways it makes us feel, tantalizing so many of our senses. When we are doing them we do not realize how much time has passed for we are so engrossed in what we are doing, so present in the Now, that nothing else actually matters for that fulfilling moment in time.

This is why children typically have no concept of time. Time becomes irrelevant when children are in that moment of total happiness and bliss, enjoying their favorite toy, game, or activity. They are using all of their senses and become totally immersed in the whole experience. This is the essence of our inner Child coming through our very own experience of all that we participate in that 'lights us up'. This is why we have no fear as we are so comfortable and happy doing what we are doing, whether it is scientific, sporty, creative,

or technical. Whatever its nature, there is a *passion* that is driving it, that burning desire to be absorbed and so incredibly elated with the activity itself no matter what the outcome is. We do not care if we succeed or if we fail. Failure inspires us to get up and try again. Success gives us the hunger to continue and strive for more success, building our belief system and our courage to just keep going.

We are surrounded by many opportunities to explore what lights us up. We just have to be intrigued and motivated enough to try all that we can. For some of us, we are able to find our spark of motivation that draws us to our passions, igniting that fire in our belly to continue to try and succeed, and if we don't succeed we just try again. For some of us, that spark is so dim and paralyzed by fear that we find it difficult to move in any direction. This is when we need to go deep into our Core, our Sacred Space, and really listen to our inner Child. We need to remember our brave self when we were a child, not over-thinking but following our heart and our gut instinct. This is so crucial to our 'being'.

We need to remember this part of us, using our instinct
to hone into what lifts our Spirit and ignites a passion,
a burning desire to do what makes our Soul truly sing
with so much joy, freedom, and a sense of Purpose.

There is no right or wrong when it comes to what we love to do or be a part of. How can there be? We are all so different. We discover our gifts and bloom at different times. And Nature is the same. Flowers and fruit only bloom when they are ready and cannot be forced. There is no set time frame or rules to adhere to for any of us. The only prerequisite is that the 'conditions' around us are in alignment with every stepping stone we dare to tread on, helping us to transform and evolve at the right moment so that we can shine so brightly when the time is right for us. It is governed by divine timing, not pressures from outside sources, including other people, or even ourselves. It is governed by all that we Dream of and commit to with all our heart and Soul.

Some of our passions can be ignited at a very early age, and some can spark very late in life. No matter what the timing is, it is important to recognize those amazing feelings that are firing and whether they bring your mind, body, and spirit to a happy place of pure enjoyment and even amazement. This is where our mindset needs to be, where we stay in the Now and continue to attract more positivity, lighting our path through what lights us up, following our passions which continue to point us to our Soul Purpose.

11 THIS IS THE MOMENT

We have an important role to play on this Earth. We <u>all</u> do. Every person is an integral cog that continues to cause this Wheel of Life to turn and it turns so well when we all work in unison, playing our part, for there isn't one person who is more important than the other. We all have an amazing part in this overall story, especially our own Story. This is the Story that matters most all, of course.

And when we focus on our Story, including our passions, our path, with our Divine Wisdom leading us on this incredible journey, we continue to point to our true North, following our Dream that ignites our Soul, keeping our inner Child alive and in awe with all life has to offer.

And as we continue to thrive in our Golden Ray of Light that continues to nurture our Soul, keeping our energy in a beautiful high vibration of attracting positivity, we are able to maximize the abundance of goodness that comes to us, whether it be gracious people, astounding opportunities, good fortune, and health. This is the ultimate in happiness and freedom, no longer a victim to the opinions of others and the vicious cycle of conformity and disharmony.

You have the power to shine and be so free in your skin, your beautiful vessel, sailing so many adventures across this beautiful planet.

You are all that you need to be, all that you are.

You are full of endless gifts and 'light bulb moments'.

You have the capacity to be so happy and full of wonder if you take the time to go out in Nature; 'feel' all there is to feel to bring your inner Child's senses alive.

It's time to fuel our senses. Find a quiet spot, preferably outside in Nature so that you can go to your special and Sacred Space.

Sit comfortably and allow yourself to breathe. Slowly take a breath in and slowly release it, and continue to breathe deeply as you go deeper and deeper inside yourself, into your Sacred Space calming your mind, your doubting Ego, as you breathe in the beautiful fresh air that surrounds you and just allow the gentle and healing sun to touch your skin, that beautiful Golden Ray of Light, so nurturing in so many ways. Allow yourself to stay in your Sacred Space for some time, for time is irrelevant, and listen to your inner Child, showing you memories of what ignites your Soul. Think about all that you have done, all that you have experienced that made you so happy, so full of wonder and so alive. So calming and so soothing to see these snapshots of you . . . just being you. This is You. This is your Soul. This is your true essence. This is where you feel most at 'home'. Take this moment to breathe it in, feel your essence with every breath. Take this moment for yourself . . . feel it. Feel You. This is the moment. And when you are ready, open your eyes and hold on to that wonderful feeling of all that is you.

We are a collection of wonderful and inspiring moments that occur every day of our lives, always experiencing and learning, seeing new ideas and miracles if we *choose* to see them. However, everything we experience is determined by how we *choose* to perceive it and this choice determines if it is a good experience or a bad experience. This experience then becomes subject to being *labeled* with various words that give it power and an emotional attachment.

If it's a good experience we will choose happy, exciting and mostly positive words.

> "That task was pretty challenging, but I stuck to it and found a solution. I actually learned something from it that I could use to get me through the next one. I am really proud of myself."

> "My coach trains me hard. He encourages me to exceed my limits and keep bettering myself with such passion and enthusiasm for each training session. He makes me feel like I can conquer anything."

If it's a bad experience we will choose negative and sometimes distressing or toxic words.

> "That task was so hard. It was such a waste of time and made me feel stupid."

> "My coach yells at me and forces me to do all this stuff every training session that is just ridiculous. He is such a cranky old man and makes me feel like I'm not good enough."

How we label our experience forms an 'opinion' of our experience that ultimately shapes our self-belief system. We can, therefore, choose to see our experiences as being all positive, for we know that what appears to be a bad snapshot or memory is really a lesson buried somewhere in that experience, helping us to become stronger, resilient, and wiser. Although the *emotions* that we felt at the time were negative, it is how we interpret the situation and label it afterward that makes a huge difference to whether the experience was actually negative, affecting our self-belief system and ultimately the vibrations that we emit to the Universe.

No matter how old the memory or experience is, we always have the opportunity to dissect and re-label it with a better understanding, a valuable lesson, that is to our benefit and not our detriment. When we change our perspective to one of positivity we release our negative emotional attachment, change our energy, and our belief system, which ultimately changes how we view our self and, in turn, allows us to really 'feel' the essence of who we are.

> **We have a chance to re-write our Story and remove the confines that were once there.**

> **We can set ourselves free from burdensome thoughts and feelings.**

> **We are able to re-structure our outlook on *everything*.**

It simply starts with a change in thought, a ripple that initiates immeasurable change. *This is the moment*. The moment where you can re-write 'what was' into a story of wonder, understanding, contentment, and freedom.

> **This is the moment that you become the master of your thoughts and the creator of your Dreams.**

12 FEAR IS AN ILLUSION

Fear is only what you *feed* it. It has no substance if you ignore it. However, the 'monster' continues to grow the more attention you give it and can grow so out of proportion that it disables your ability to function . . . if you *let* it.

This 'monster' lives in the imagination of our Ego. It is a story we tend to create and continue to embellish as we continue to play the story, or our version of the 'recording', over and over in our minds. We continue to add bits and pieces to our 'monster' until we no longer see it as a collection of information that we have simply fuelled with the incorrect emotion that was started by *discomfort*.

Discomfort is not a bad thing. It only functions as information to your body that you are not happy with a certain situation that has disrupted your comfort zone, or you are dissatisfied with a certain person that is negatively intruding on your senses. It is how we decide to *interpret* the discomfort and with what emotion we *attach* to it that determines whether we are going to deal with it or not.

So many of us do get caught up in the emotion that we have attached to our experience, especially when we play back what we have recorded in our mind over and over, attaching anxiety or anger to it. Then we tend to fast forward to only certain parts of this occurrence and stay focused, or even fixated, on these particular parts. We continue to fuel those parts with more negative emotions until it becomes something or someone that we want to avoid, for to avoid them lessens our overall level of emotion and what ultimately becomes a much higher level of discomfort. However, to avoid what gives us a very high level of discomfort can then lead to inhibiting our ability to function when we are faced with the same situations or types of people, as we tend to 'globalize' them and thus create a 'fear'.

So the more we focus on certain parts of the occurrence, re-live the discomfort of our sensations and label them with negative emotions, the more we tend to feed our 'monster' and embody the story we have told ourselves with fear. If we are the creator of our Story that we tell ourselves, then we are also the creator of our 'monster' in that Story, hence we are the creator of our fear.

If we create and *give power* to our fear,
we are also able to *disable* that fear.

There are moments when our fears are extremely paralyzing so we are not in control of our emotions or the sensations in our body that overwhelm and overtake our inner Wisdom. We are not aware of our inner Voice or our Warrior within. We have lost focus on all that is good and the fact that we are actually okay. If we are not in immediate physical danger, then the only other situation we are in is up in our head and being controlled by our Ego. Our mind becomes disarrayed with insignificant information that is not logical or rational because our fear has escalated to extreme levels.

Obviously, this is not healthy for us, or even those around us, for 'fear' can also be a learned behavior. For instance, many of us have a fear of dogs, spiders, or snakes because we have learned this fear sometimes through a bad experience, but usually because we have learned this fear from an adult during our childhood. We have been told not to touch or go near this animal as it will hurt us in some way. For example, we are told that it will bite, sting or, poison us. Though we may not have experienced a negative situation ourselves, we believe the adult about the outcome depending on the strength of the relationship and the influence the adult has on us, incorporating this information into our belief system. It is embedded in our Core and can grow to unhealthy proportions. The irrational information based on hear-say, like most information passed through society (parents, school, religion, etc.), has not been questioned or dissected, therefore not discarded in time. This is why we need to follow our inner Child and experience more, gathering the information for ourselves and using this information to build our self-belief system based on our facts, not emotion, hence growing our strength, courage, resilience, and determination to face and conquer our deceptive fears.

By dealing with the occurrence and dissecting it into parts, without labeling it with negative emotions, we can simplify it and assess the information at hand. It is when we are consumed by emotion that we become distracted and even 'blinded' because we do not have all the facts. We can sift through this information in our Sacred Space, our Core, focusing on a solution and how we are going to reach this solution; which tools we have, and what tools we can attain from others (that being those that come from a place of love and compassion).

Rather than feed that monster, we continue to fuel our self-belief that we will find a solution. And when we do find it and it proves successful, we have nurtured our Inner Warrior once again and proven that *fear is nothing more than an illusion*.

13 TIME TO SHINE

This is your moment to shine bright and be a beacon to those that are around you. You do not have to be the best at everything. You just have to do the best you can do when you are doing the thing that sets your Soul on fire, the thing that lights your senses and fuels you to keep striving until you get there.

The destination does not have to be up high, or very far, it just has to be a place that makes you so very happy and exalted in your Core, in your heart. You may have many goals and destinations that you reach along your path, which makes the journey more interesting, more exciting. You may not get there smoothly. You may even get misguided and confused along the way, but if we continue to listen to our inner Voice and stand in the Golden Ray of Light, we will accomplish so much more than we ever dreamed we could.

So many of us seem to get lost along our journey simply because we dare not to be 'seen'. We are constantly ducking and weaving, dodging the doubts and disparities cast by others, not wanting to be in

their sights in fear of being ridiculed, humiliated or much worse . . . of being *rejected*. It is common behavior for many of us to remain in the background and to turn down our Light until it eventually is snuffed out. This does not serve our Purpose nor does it serve our wellbeing. We have become lost in society's controlling ways of diminishing those who stand tall and achieve. We have lost our courage to simply be ourselves.

Every star in the night sky shines brightly. There is not one star that hides its light. Every star draws on its inner Core, radiating its true inner Source, adding to the energy of the Universe . . . just continuing to *shine*. There is no competition, ridicule, or negativity amongst them all. They all play their own part whatever that may be. There is no judgment or opinions cast. They all just co-exist in harmony.

When we all learn to shine our Light, we are radiating love, happiness, and positive vibes on every level.

This can only create a ripple effect of more of the same. We attract what we emit, and repel what we don't. So we should be conscious of doing what makes us happy, what gives the Light inside us an endless Source of fuel.

This Light inside us is also what attracts our Tribe, which are those souls that also live, breathe, and feel the same about those things that mean so much to us. This group of people that love what we love are our People. They are the ones that evolve with us, helping us to achieve our goals as we continue to walk our path, helping others along the way, holding out the Light of Compassion, accepting ourselves, and accepting others as we recognize ourselves in them and vice versa.

Trying to fit into a group that does not share our beliefs and ideals only makes us relinquish all that we are including our inner Light, our Warrior within. We stop standing tall, we change and *lower* our beliefs about ourselves and we continue to diminish and dissolve into someone insignificant and not worthy of being noticed, accepted, and loved. This is a poor and shallow existence.

Finding our Tribe means that we need to shine brightly so that they can find us. After all, *like attracts like*. Take this moment to think of all the people that are in your life, your world.

Do they lift and inspire you?

Do they support your ideas, your Dreams, and overall wellbeing?

Do they love and support you unconditionally, helping you to find ways to reach your goals and succeed?

If you answered 'Yes' to all of these questions then these people are part of your Tribe. Those that are continually negative, bringing you and your aspirations down, constantly draining your positive energy to the point of toxicity are <u>not</u> your Tribe, even if they are family or close friends. It is harder to change your family than it is to change your circle of friends, so it is all about training your inner Warrior to be more proficient in guarding your energy with the Golden Ray of light and to strengthen your internal muscle of sifting and dissecting, being quite specific as to what criteria you uphold in allowing what enters and stays within your Sacred Space and ultimately becomes a part of your self-belief system, your Core.

We do not have to allow the negative opinions of others into our self-belief system. We have the choice, the power, to accept these opinions or to reject them. It takes strength, courage, and resilience to realize who is part of our Tribe and who is not. And for those who are not, we need to strengthen our outer armor, our Golden Bubble of Protection and, in turn, shower them in the Golden Ray of Light also in an attempt to reduce their negativity and possible toxicity. We also have the power to minimize our interaction with such people. We need to put our strategies in place, allowing the Warrior within to continue to step forward to protect our Core and optimize peace within our environment wherever possible. This will assist in self-preservation of the Light you shine to the world around you.

You have a duty of care to look after your adventurous inner Child and your wise Ancient One so that you can shine bright and continue to attract your Tribe. There is no room for anything or anyone other than those that help you to be the best version of you that you can be and to shine brightly. Your Tribe, in essence, is your 'family' on many levels, whether you are related to them or not. They are a community of sharing, a people of compassion, Warriors of Wisdom also shining their Light for the good of all. They are 'home'. By attracting your Tribe you can only be more of You and true to who you are. If you haven't found them already then it *is time to shine*.

14 STAY TRUE TO YOURSELF

There is no need to continually dim your light to fit in and please others.

There is no need to constantly suppress your deepest wishes and Dreams.

You are a shining Light that has so much to offer the world as well as to those people that *appreciate* you and *accept* you for who you are.

**You have the power to shine so brightly
just by embracing all parts that are you and
smiling from the inside out.**

This true smile only comes to the surface when we are beaming our true Source of energy from within, when we are truly enjoying the moment of doing what makes us insurmountably happy . . . what lights us up.

This is who we are, every fiber of our being. This is where we are truly meant to be, just shining our Light. And when we do, our Light inspires others to shine their Light. It is an endless ripple effect of one candle lighting the other until we create a sea of Light . . . or a Universe of Stars.

As we continue to sparkle from the depths of our heart singing our Song, a Song unique to each and every one of us, just like the whales of the ocean calling their mate or their tribe, we continue to emit our individual Source of energy that is at its peak when we are full of compassion and Love, when we are true to who we are, disregarding the 'white noise' around us, keeping our energy clean and strong with the Golden Ray of Light.

As we continue to draw on the Golden Ray of Light we are able to protect our beautiful and precious energy so we do not resonate with the negative but continue to attract Love and Light. We are able to cleanse our vessel and discard all that is toxic, all limiting beliefs, and continue to shine this Golden Light wherever we are to keep our vibration high.

As we continue to draw the Golden Ray of Light within us, we diminish the negative, the doubt, and the illusion of fear. We continue to be our own source of energy, shining brighter and brighter. We continue to blaze so brilliantly that we find our Tribe, just as the Ancient Ones did long ago, building their community, their People, supporting one another, their strengths, their gifts, and their Dreams.

There is no 'room' whenever you are trying to just 'fit in'. It is never comfortable nor a perfect fit and you always feel like you are still on the outside. It is a constant shift of existence to non-existence, from feeling safe to ultimately feeling bored, for to just travel a road that is not part of your journey does not allow you to bare your Soul and reveal who you really are. You begin to fade into the background and become part of the 'white noise', not really belonging just drifting. This is not Life. This is social conditioning . . . an epidemic of destruction to our Light.

If we continue to dim our Light to fit in, we continue to feel discomfort which leads to fear, anxiety, depression, and anger, to a feeling of hopelessness, unworthiness and not ever feeling like we are good enough because we are trying to please others, living to their standards, rules, and expectations.

We only need to take one step at a time along our Golden Path of Synchronicity and continue to add to our collection of Pearls of Wisdom.

We only need to do what makes us happy so that there is a ripple effect of happiness generated to those that care for and love us unconditionally, our Tribe.

We do not need to 'fit in' and suffer from various levels of discomfort, fear, and negativity which only leads us down a path of destruction.

The only way we can protect ourselves from destruction is to just believe in ourselves, all that we are, all that we love, and all that lights us up. Simply said, *stay true to yourself*.

15 HEART OF GOLD

Some generations before us, there was a time when a fearful and ego-filled minority began to feed the rest of us with so much fear and misinformation in order to dominate us. We were starved of the Truth. We were deprived of a free Spirit that was so natural and so connected to the essence of Mother Nature. We were made to conform to harsh rules that no longer allowed us to even 'connect' with each other. It still continues today.

We had so much strength and unity back in the days when we were all part of a community of people that gave so much to each other. We were a community that shared our Light, our essence, just as the Ancient Ones did long ago. We did not covet possessions, we did not put another down nor shun them because of their differences. We were a People that respected all that were in our Tribe. We were a People that loved all that the Great Creator gifted us with – always grateful, always giving back to the Land and to each other.

Surrounding ourselves with people who lift and light our Light is essential to follow our path. We cannot live in isolation but we can choose our Tribe. We all radiate, reflect, and absorb Light from one another, shining so

brightly when we reach euphoric states of mind, body, and spirit.

Down below the Earth's surface is an energy that also radiates from the core of the planet, giving life and synchronicity to all inhabitants. All of us rely on this energy, Mother Nature's energy, spreading through the ecosystems, so precise and balanced when Man does not interfere with the intricacies of every relationship and system. We too are an ecosystem of our own, our internal systems operating so precisely and in balance if we allow them to be. As the Earth revolves around the sun, our body revolves around our tireless beating heart, giving force to our mind, body, and spirit. Giving us the inner Wisdom from our Ancient One. Giving us the courage from our inner Child to explore as well as the strength to survive and succeed from our growing Warrior within.

So much comes from our heart. It plays such a vital and strategic role in our existence and our Soul Purpose, continuing to propel our life force, our Source, and our Love. It is precious on so many levels. It is truly a *heart of gold*.

Come into your heart, your Soul. There you will find your inner strength and power, the force that drives you to succeed, to Love, and be happy.

This heart is full of goodness and has so much Love to give. It is the essence of who you are. It holds the key to so many doors that are around you. It is the whole essence of your existence and holds all of your Dreams.

You are the keeper of your heart and you are also the guardian. You have a duty to take care of it, nourish it, and above all to keep your heart's Light shining bright. You have all that you need to keep it burning bright, emitting energy so pure and so full of Love.

What you put into your heart, your Core, your Sacred Space, can only be of benefit to your wellbeing. Do not sacrifice this Space for others who do not respect your talents, your beliefs and your Dreams. Stay true to yourself, and fill this Space with those beautiful things you have stored in your beautiful treasure chest in the Temple of Gold, that are the fuel to your essence, allowing the Golden Ray of Light to continue to flow within

and around you.

You are full of treasures and you are full of miracles just waiting to happen.

You are full of amazing ideas and creativity.

You are full of endless energy from God, Source, the Universe . . . the Golden Ray of Light.

ABOUT HELEN

Helen Lauritzen is the author of 'No Grit, No Pearl' - the first book in the 'Warrior Of Wisdom' series.

Drawing on her natural therapies background of being a Reiki Master and Teacher, as well as a color therapist, Helen is passionate about sharing her gifts and knowledge with others to significantly enhance their health and wellbeing.

Being intuitive from an infant, she has always had a strong connection to the Universe and her divine guides, sharing their Wisdom and messages with those in need. Her books, filled with beautiful messages and illustrations, are their gift to you.

"I hope this book has given you the tools to cleanse, protect and always shine your Light. May you continue to strengthen your Inner Warrior of Wisdom with the Golden Ray Of Light as well as follow your heart, your Soul, and your Dreams. ♥ "

Next book in Warrior of Wisdom series:

Book 3 – One Tribe

www.ingramcontent.com/pod-product-compliance
Lightning Source LLC
LaVergne TN
LVHW072106070426
835509LV00002B/36